THEN & NOW®

DENTON

OPPOSITE: The 1896 Denton County Courthouse-on-the-Square is considered one of the finest historical courthouses in Texas with its soaring clock tower reaching 140 feet into the Texas sky. The building's Richardsonian Romanesque architectural style features 82 Burnet County red granite columns with caps and bases of Pecos Red sandstone and walls constructed of tan sandstone from Mineral Wells. (Courtesy of Denton County Museums.)

THEN & NOW®

DENTON

Kim Cupit

and Dr. Georgia Caraway

For all the descendants of pioneer families and the newcomers who call Denton, Texas, home. And to the memory of Bob Caraway, who represents the past of our lives, and to Zoe Noelle, who is our future.

ISBN 978-0-7385-8518-5

Library of Congress Control Number: 2011928538

Published by Arcadia Publishing
Charleston, South Carolina

Printed in the United States of America

For all general information, please contact Arcadia Publishing:
Telephone 843-853-2070
Fax 843-853-0044
E-mail sales@arcadiapublishing.com
For customer service and orders:
Toll-Free 1-888-313-2665

Visit us on the Internet at www.arcadiapublishing.com

On the Front Cover: The Denton Square has always been a busy hub of activity, whether it is with horse-drawn wagons, trolleys, or automobiles. Finding a parking space has remained a challenge for downtown visitors. These photographs were taken in 1958 on the east side of the square and again in 2011. Some things never change. (Then image courtesy of *Denton Record-Chronicle* archives at the Denton County Museums, now image courtesy of Carl Oberman.)

On the Back Cover: The Denton County seat was moved from its first location in Pinckneyville to an area three miles southeast named Alton, which is now the present town of Corinth. Due to a lack of water, the county seat moved again to Hickory Creek. This site was also called Alton. This hunting party is in front of the tree that served as the site for court in the 1840s in Alton. (Courtesy of Wayne and Melbagene Ryan.)

Contents

ACKNOWLEDGMENTS

Kim and I had some concerns about writing a third pictorial history book about Denton. The question we posed to ourselves was, "Can we make this book different and interesting enough and tell more of the history of the city without repeating what we had already done in the previous two Denton history books?" It wasn't until we started finding these photographs and researching their stories that our fears were set aside. The selected photographs in this book show a whole different perspective of Denton's history. And the fun adventure of discovering the city's evolution into what it is now was an added bonus.

Heartfelt thanks go to the *Denton Record-Chronicle* (DRC) and the Patterson family for donating the newspaper's photographic archive to the Denton County Museums (DCM), the Denton Public Library (DPL) for allowing us to use their vintage photographs, the University of North Texas Archives (UNT), the City of Denton, Louise Vanderhoff, Alec Williams, Greg D. Hubbard, Lucile Rayzor Hutchinson, Charline Scripture Rodgers, David Martino, Dottie Holliday, Jim Bolz, Smith and Etha Kiker, Mike Cochran, Dr. Johnnie Myers, Don Epperson, Melvena Noles, Eddie Cates, *Hartlee Times*, Wayne and Melbagene Ryan, Richard Calo'oy and Steve Watkins of Prop & Lens Aerial Photo-Graphics for the contemporary aerial photographs, photographer Squire Haskins for his historic aerial shots, the Arcadia staff for encouraging us to do the book, and Natasha, Gretel, and Robyn of the Denton County Museums staff for keeping the museums running while we worked on this book. As always, we appreciate the support of the Denton County Commissioners Court, the Denton County Historical Commission and Roslyn Shelton, and the Denton County Museums Committee. All vintage photographs are from the Denton County Museums archives unless otherwise noted.

The greatest volunteer effort was performed by photographer extraordinaire Carl Oberman, who took all the modern photographs as a gift to the Museums. We could not have created this book without him. Thank you, Carl, for your patience, your time, and your exceptional talent.

Introduction

Denton has grown from a rustling frontier town to a bustling city. Founded in 1857 as the fourth county seat of Denton County, Denton occupies the geographic center of the county. The additions of the Texas and Pacific and the Missouri-Kansas-Texas Railroads in the 1880s, the University of North Texas in 1890 and Texas Woman's University in 1903, and the east and west branches of Interstate 35 in the 1950s and 1960s have contributed to the development of the city.

Denton residents have been conducting business on the square for over 150 years. Shortly after Sheriff C.A. Williams auctioned off the new city lots in January 1857, construction began on the new town square. A log courthouse was erected facing Oak Street on the north side of the square. Until the late 1870s, the structures were primarily made of wood, making them susceptible to fire. That courthouse burned during Christmas 1875 and a new brick courthouse was built in the center of the square the following year. By the 1880s, Denton truly had become the center of the county. The Texas and Pacific and Missouri-Kansas-Texas Railroads both ran through Denton, making goods readily available. The square became home to a variety of locally-owned businesses. Several buildings built during the last two decades of the 19th century survive today. During the mid-20th century, the square became a mix of locally-owned and chain stores. Duke & Ayers, Beall's, and J.C. Penney's were a few of the national chains that occupied the old buildings. As more residents began driving, parking became an increasing problem on the square. By 1960, grocery stores had completely disappeared from the square, choosing to build a couple of blocks away where parking was more ample. After the Denton Center was built on University Drive, more businesses moved from the square. Despite competition from other areas of town, the downtown square continued to thrive. As they could 150 years ago, Denton residents can venture to the square to get legal advice, buy furniture, shop for clothing, grab a bite to eat, and get a drink.

Longtime residents have seen many things come and go in Denton. Many historic buildings were lost during the mid to late 20th century in the name of progress. Neighborhoods located in close proximity to the downtown square were razed to make room for businesses. Historic homes were lost to development and apartment buildings constructed to house the growing student population. The primary business district shifted from downtown to University Drive and then again to Loop 288. Other structures have fallen victim to fire and new buildings have been built from the ashes.

Organizations such as the Historic Landmark Commission and the Denton County Historical Commission have ensured that many of Denton's old buildings have been preserved. The historical 1896 Courthouse-on-the-Square became overcrowded in the 1970s and county offices moved to the Carroll Courts Building in 1978. County officials ensured that the building would be saved. After two renovations, the building currently houses the Courthouse-on-the-Square Museum, the Denton County Historical Commission, the Commissioners Court, and the offices of the County Judge and Commissioners.

Denton continues to be an active city hosting annual events such as the Arts and Jazz Festival and Dog Days of Denton. The North Texas State Fair and Rodeo has provided quality western entertainment for the last 83 years. Denton is also the home of the Denton County Museums, which operates two facilities, the aforementioned Courthouse-on-the-Square Museum and the Historical Park of Denton County. The Historical Park features structures that would otherwise have been lost to development or neglect, including the Bayless-Selby House Museum and the award-winning Denton County African American Museum. The Denton County Historical Commission is continually restoring other buildings to make them available for visitors.

Those fortunate to call Denton home remember the past and look forward to an extraordinary future.

CHAPTER 1

East Side, West Side, All Around Town

Denton, Texas, was a frontier prairie town at the time this photograph of the west side of the Denton downtown square was taken in 1876. By the next decade, the Wild West appearance of the structures would be modernized by brick facades.

This panoramic 1918 photograph of Denton Square's north side shows thriving businesses including grocery stores, cafes, a bank, a photography studio, a furniture/undertaking business, and the Benevolent and Protective Order of Elks (BPOE) Lodge No. 807 in the May Building. The center of the block

was built in the 1880s. The three businesses of McNeill's Appliances, Thomas' Ethan Allen, and McBride Music and Pawn have operated in their current locations since the 1960s. McNeill's, the oldest of these retailers, has been in business since the 1930s.

The Lacy Hotel was built in 1858, one year after the lots were laid out for the city of Denton. The wooden hotel burned in 1884, and a brick structure, the May Building, was built in its place. Fire destroyed the May Building in 1924, and the structure was replaced by the Smoot-Curtis Building. In the early 1950s, Robert Morris purchased the building and changed its title to reflect his name. The building changed ownership several more times and is now known as the Texas Building. (Courtesy of DRC.)

The Wright Opera House, built in 1899 with the bricks of the 1876 courthouse, showcased vaudevillian and opera stars until it closed in 1913. During the next 76 years, the building housed Parlin and Orendorff Implement Company, the Boston Store, and Kibler Office Supplies. The building now houses Recycled Books, Records, and CDs in the basement, first floor, and mezzanine and seven loft apartments on the second and third floors. (Courtesy of DPL.)

This 1903 photograph is of the fire department during a drill on West Oak Street a block off the square. The Arcade was a large furniture store situated to the east of the fire station and city hall. Sue's Formal Gowns, the Labb Sports Bar and Lounge, and United & Holland Mattress Company currently occupy the block.

These 1920s automobiles made their way west from the Ritz Theatre, past Edwards & McCrary Furniture at 218 West Oak Street and Denton Dairy Products at 220 West Oak Street, to the intersection at Bolivar Street. Today, cars travel the same route from Andy's Bar, passing restaurants, coffee bars, nightclubs featuring art and live music, vintage and formal wear clothing shops, and art studios, ending at United & Holland Mattress Company.

This early 1900s view of East Oak Street was taken from the intersection of Oakland Street and the square. Many of Denton's first residences were built in close proximity to the downtown square. Victorian-style homes lined the street before the area was taken over by businesses and apartments.

This 1876 brick structure served as the county courthouse until it was condemned and then torn down in 1895. The 1896 courthouse was built on the same site. A new four-story courthouse at 1450 East McKinney Street was dedicated in 1998. It houses courtrooms, offices for the county's attorneys and judges, the county and district clerks, records management, and print/mail.

The west side of Denton's square, as shown in this 1918 panoramic view, catered to patrons seeking furniture, drugs, books and sundries, and dry goods. Today, visitors can find fine jewelry,

attend church, eat home-style meals, buy home decorative items and antiques, have a will drawn, or visit the UNT on the Square art gallery.

The Elm Street side of the square was nicknamed Theatre Row after the Dreamland opened in 1913, the Palace in 1922, and the Texas in 1935. Deanna Durbin and Mickey Rooney starred in *That Certain Age* at the Texas in this 1938 photograph. The Fine Arts Theatre took over the Texas Theatre in 1957 and is now the home of a church.

Although the Fine Arts building remains on Elm Street, as shown in this 1965 photograph, no operational theater remains on the square today. Shrader's Pharmacy, one of Denton's oldest drugstores, operated from 1944 until 1998. Western Auto, located in the historical Scripture Building, was another mainstay on the square. (Then photograph by Greg D. Hubbard.)

The south side of the square on Hickory Street burned in 1877, destroying all of the businesses. Another fire destroyed the Raley Building in the center of the block in 1972. The Evers Hardware building, built in 1913, is one of the most recognizable structures on the

square. The family-owned business provided Denton residents with hard-to-find hardware needs until it closed in 2001. A profusion of restaurants and specialty shops occupy the block today.

The square's southwest corner, the Donahower Block, was built in 1893. When L.T. Fox, owner of Fox Hardware, sold these 1912 Fords, an attendant went with each car to teach the man of the house how to drive. The block burned in 1914. W.B. McClurkan constructed the current building in 1915. It became Russell's Department Store and is now the Hickory Street Office Building.

Parking meters line both sides of Hickory Street on the downtown square in this 1950s photograph. Parking meters were installed on the square in 1941 but barely lasted the year. They were reinstalled in September 1948. The first two weeks netted $1,335 for the city. Free parking returned in 1967 at the request of the Denton Chamber of Commerce. A two-hour limit is now being imposed. (Courtesy of DRC.)

Most of the buildings shown in this 1918 east side panoramic photograph of the square remain underneath their 1960s facades. The block is bookended by the Paschall Building on the west,

erected in 1877, and the Bank building on the east, built in 1913. Today, businesses thrive in these center-of-the-block buildings constructed after an 1890 fire that destroyed most of the block.

This 1880s view shows the Exchange National Bank and William A. Ponder home at the corner of Hickory and Locust Streets. The Bank constructed a new building at this site in 1913. First State Bank took over the southeast corner location in 1931. A new building was erected on this site in 1961 and expanded in 1972. It is now home to Wells Fargo Bank.

C. Alex Williams opened his store on Locust Street next door to the Denton County National Bank in 1899. Will Williams took over management of the store upon his father's death and sold the business in 1956. After many years of being concealed under plaster, the original bricks were uncovered to make way for North Texas Foot and Ankle Specialists and four apartments. (Courtesy of DRC.)

Gas stations popped up at the corner of North Locust and East McKinney Streets to service the increased automobile traffic in Denton. In the interest of progress, these businesses were torn down to make way for a new post office in 1975. The original 1919 post office served the public for 55 years. A stunning view of Texas Woman's University is in the background of both pictures. (Courtesy of DRC.)

Several former Denton businesses and industries can be seen in this 1960s aerial photograph. Robert Thomas Harpool Sr. and his son Tom opened R.T. Harpool & Sons at the corner of McKinney Street and Bell Avenue in 1939. Harpool's was sold in 1998 and remodeled as restaurant and retail space. The Texas & Pacific Railroad (T&P) Depot, seen near the train tracks, was torn down in 1964. The flour mill burned in 1967. (Then photograph courtesy of City of Denton and Squire Haskins, now photograph courtesy of Prop & Lens.)

Power Plant no. 2 was built in 1947 and abandoned in the 1970s. The empty shell remained unoccupied until the building was renovated in 2003 by Kirkpatrick Architecture Studio for the Central Fire Station, a city construction project reflecting adaptive reuse. (Courtesy of Alec Williams.)

The interior of the abandoned city power plant had floor to ceiling windows allowing plenty of light, which encouraged a tree to grow in the dirt floor. Part of the adaptive reuse project created a fireman's museum featuring vintage firefighting equipment and accoutrement. The museum was established through the efforts of Denton firefighters who wanted to share the distinguished history of their line of work. (Courtesy of City of Denton.)

The City of Denton created its first public park after purchasing and removing the African American community of Quakertown in the early 1920s. The city built a playground, swimming pool, and baseball field on the park grounds. The park was renamed Quakertown Park in 2009. The rock bridge, constructed by WPA workers in 1938, spans Pecan Creek connecting the Woman's Club Building with the park. (Courtesy of DPL.)

Denton City Hall, located at 221 North Elm Street, was dedicated by Gov. Dan Moody on October 8, 1927. This Spanish Renaissance building was the seat of city government until 1967 when the new city hall was built on McKinney Street. Denton-educated and noted Texas architect O'Neil Ford designed the new building, which still serves as the main administrative building for municipal government. (Courtesy of DPL.)

Denton Hospital and Clinic was constructed in 1925 on South Locust Street at a cost of $35,000. It was described as a "modern institution for the diagnosis and treatment of medical, surgical and obstetrical cases." The hospital contained 35 patient rooms and a chartered training school for nurses. It closed as a hospital on December 31, 1955. The building underwent extensive renovations in 2002 and was purchased in 2007 to be the headquarters for Nuconsteel.

Moore Business Forms was founded in 1882 by Samuel J. Moore. The Southern Division Home Office moved to Denton in 1947. Moore Business Forms was the world's largest manufacturer of business forms and machines. The Denton plant closed in 1987. The City of Denton purchased the building in 1990 and converted it into City Hall East, housing the police department and city jail, municipal court, and other city departments. (Courtesy of DPL.)

The expansion of northern Carroll Boulevard to Highway 24 (now Highway 380) began in 1970, creating a bottleneck where the improvements ended at Mulberry Street. Residents of and visitors to the city sighed in relief when the southern widening and rerouting of this north-south thoroughfare was finally completed in 1978. (Courtesy of Alec Williams.)

The Carroll Courts Building served as the county courthouse from 1978 until 1998. When the new courts building opened, this building was converted into county administrative offices for budget, purchasing, payroll, auditing, county treasurer, technology services, elections, human resources, Justice of the Peace Precinct 1, and Constable Precinct 1. (Courtesy of DPL.)

Denton's Industrial Street was an early haven for small-town businesses when Wolf's Food Store and Denton Farm and Ranch Supply occupied the block. The street has undergone a renaissance in the last 10 years with the addition of award-winning, diverse businesses such as Seniors in Motion, Dan's Silverleaf, Fuzzy's Taco Shop, and Rooster's Roadhouse. The revitalization efforts on this end of East Hickory Street have created an indie music and casual dining destination in downtown. (Courtesy of DRC.)

Denton Center was the first available shopping plaza outside of downtown Denton when it opened in 1960. Customers found the convenience of a drugstore, supermarket, clothing shop, a variety store, barbershop, a cafeteria, and national-chain department stores. The center offers similar neighborhood services today. (Courtesy of DRC.)

This shopping center has always catered to the students and neighborhoods surrounding the University of North Texas campus. It provided in the 1970s, and still provides today, convenience to banking, restaurants, thrift stores, and personal care salons. Early residents may remember Buddies Supermarket and Gibson's Discount Center. Buildings of Denton's two universities can be seen in the background. (Then photograph courtesy of DRC, now photograph courtesy of Prop & Lens.)

This 1960s photograph shows Interstate Highway 35E traveling south when the acreage on both sides of the highway was open farmland. Although the highway is taken for granted or cursed for its traffic snarls today, it was declared a vision come true when dedicated in 1960. This vital connection between Dallas and Denton has contributed to the growth of Denton. Three of the city's strongest features are its location, its universities, and its excellent highway system. (Then photograph courtesy of DPL and Squire Haskins, now photograph courtesy of Prop & Lens.)

The University of North Texas Administration Building was constructed in 1956 with the McConnell Memorial Tower that houses a carillon and a set of Westminster chimes. It still stands as a centerpiece for the ever-expanding campus. From the original 10-acre site to campuses in Dallas and Fort Worth, the university has become an internationally known public research institution. (Courtesy of DPL.)

CHAPTER 2

PLACES TO REMEMBER

The Town and Country Drive-in opened as the Rancho on Highway 77 in 1948. This popular gathering place provided entertainment under the stars on hot Texas summer nights. This photograph was taken in 1987 after the "T&C" closed and fell to neglect. Evidence of the poles that held car window speakers sprout out of the ground among the weeds and overgrown grass. (Courtesy of DRC.)

The Robert E. Lee School opened in the fall of 1909 at the site of the former Central School. In 1923, a new building replaced the older structure. Lee Elementary School moved to Mack Place in 1974. The old building was demolished and is now the location of the expansion of the First United Methodist Church and its parking lot. (Courtesy of Alec Williams.)

Stonewall Jackson School first opened in 1899 on Gary Street as the North Ward School. After the structure burned in 1916, a new building was constructed. The school was phased out in 1982–1983. Much to the dismay of former students, the beloved Stonewall Jackson School was torn down in 1986 to make way for the Denton Independent School District Central Services building. (Courtesy of Alec Williams.)

Sam Houston School, also called West Ward School, was built in 1905 on Welch Street near the North Texas State Normal College. The school closed in 1974, and the current Sam Houston Elementary School opened on Teasley Lane in 1982. The University of North Texas purchased the structure, using it as a classroom laboratory until it was replaced by a parking garage in 1986.

This white Colonial-style home was constructed on Eagle Drive in 1956. For the next 43 years, the house served as the residence for several university presidents and as the development office. It was torn down to make way for the Gateway Banquet and Conference Center, a 28,000-square-foot, multilevel facility. The Gateway Center includes meeting rooms, outdoor spaces, and an extensive banquet facility. (Courtesy of UNT.)

The Texas Woman's University (TWU) Open Air Theater opened in 1929 and offered free programs and motion pictures to students until 1950. The university still offers outdoor activities and events on the campus lawn for its students. TWU takes great pride in its gardens and landscaping. The university's interest in campus beautification and its proliferation of redbud trees contributed to Denton being named the "Redbud Capital of Texas." (Courtesy of DRC.)

In order to accommodate the growing population of students between 1918 and 1936, eight new dormitory buildings, affectionately called "dormitory row," were added to the Texas Woman's University campus on a site north of Old Main. Dormitory row was razed in the 1980s to make room for the new library. The Mary Evelyn Blagg Huey Library was dedicated in 1986 and named in honor of the first woman president of the university and the only alumna to hold that position. (Courtesy of DPL.)

J. Newton Rayzor purchased 289 acres at the corner of Bonnie Brae and Scripture Streets in 1955 to build his summer home, Hillview Ranch. The development known as Rayzor Ranch is divided by University Drive and is slated to become a multiuse retail, residential, and office complex featuring a museum and park space. (Courtesy of Lucile Rayzor Hutchinson.)

This three-story, 12-room house was built by Charles Scripture in 1901 on the site that became known as Scripture Hill. Callie Scripture chose this location because she wanted to see Denton in all directions. The house was moved across the street when Flow Memorial Hospital was constructed. Flow Hospital was torn down in 2002 to make way for the CityParc at Fry Street, which created controversy when the heirloom trees were removed during construction of the apartment complex. (Courtesy of Charline Scripture Rodgers.)

Alvin C. Owsley's lovely country home stood at 2269 West Oak Street until 1972 when it was torn down to make way for student housing, the Cluster Apartments. The multifamily construction boom of the 1970s is being repeated today, but instead of older homes being destroyed by progress, the city is losing its greenspace.

101 North Elm Street has been the site of two fires: the Great Fire of 1860, which destroyed most of the west side of the square, and the 1994 fire, which leveled what was commonly known as the Lawyers Building. The Sherman Building, erected in 1996, is a good example of infill construction that salutes the architecture surrounding it.

The large two-story home at 220 South Locust Street was owned by Martha E. Francis from the 1920s until the 1950s. The family of C.C. Bell resided next door at 210 South Locust Street. This neighborhood, one block off the square, was converted into commercial property in the late 1950s when these two homes were torn down for the expansion of Chester Morris Chevrolet. The Wells Fargo Bank drive-in occupies this space.

Sandy's was an iconic example of drive-in restaurants popular in 1960s Denton. Located on University Drive where Arby's is today, Sandy's reflected a time when cruising the strip was a popular teenage pastime. University Drive is still a hotbed of fast-food restaurants. Sonic Drive-in is the remaining example of eating fast food delivered to your car by carhops. (Courtesy of DRC.)

Controversy has surrounded the Fry Street area since the 1960s when bars, restaurants, and the Fry Street Fair provided places for students to hang out. In 2006, an outside developer purchased a portion of the block for multiuse, but the project never came to pass. Students and neighbors are looking forward to the day when the area will resonate with music and activity again. (Courtesy of Alec Williams.)

The 1891 jail on North Elm Street did not afford much privacy, so prisoners put up blankets to make their own walls. The building remained standing until 1965 when it was torn down. The first inmates moved into the Denton County Jail on Woodrow Lane in 1986. The jail originally had a 233-bed capacity. The current county jail has a capacity of 1,400 inmates and comprises five law enforcement facilities.

Russell-Newman Manufacturing Company was founded in 1939 by partners Rowe Newman and J. Holford Russell. The company's executive offices, as shown in this 1968 photograph, were located on East Hickory Street. The Black Box Performing Arts Center now occupies a renovated portion of Denton Publishing Company, which once was Russell-Newman's headquarters. The publishing company rents the space to Denton Community Theater for $1 per month. This new space also provides a training area for students who are interested in honing their craft. (Courtesy of David Martino.)

CHAPTER 3

Those Were the Days

Brooks Drugstore moved from the west side of the square to 222 West Hickory Street in 1956. The soda fountains in the many downtown drugstores were popular hangouts for teens. The last drugstore on the square closed in 1998. Beth Marie's Old Fashioned Ice Cream opened that same year to provide a new generation of Denton residents a place to grab a soda, a shake, or a sundae. (Courtesy of Dottie Holliday.)

When court was held under this tree at the 1850-to-1856 county seat of Alton, the city of Denton did not exist. The desire for a more centrally located courthouse resulted in the creation of Denton in 1857. Guyer High School, Denton's third high school, is located near the early governmental site. This blending of history with development provides a unique environment for family living.

Denton High School, designed by Wiley G. Clarkson in 1924, was located at 709 Congress Street. In 1957, the building became Congress Junior High when a new high school opened on Fulton Street. Amos O. Calhoun, the principal of the high school from 1924 to 1957, was honored in 1982 when the old building became Calhoun Middle School.

Construction was completed for the first leg of Loop 288 from Highway 77 (now Interstate 35E) to State Highway 24 (now Highway 380) in 1959. The road would expand north in 1987 and again in 1992 to eventually reach Interstate 35 north of Denton. Originally envisioned as a relief for downtown traffic, Loop 288 has had a history of traffic troubles almost since its construction, especially after the opening of the Golden Triangle Mall in 1980 and Denton Crossing Shopping Center in 2003. (Then photograph courtesy of DRC, now photograph courtesy of Prop & Lens.)

The Denton Chamber of Commerce got its start in the late 1890s as the Denton Commercial Club, meeting in the Wright Opera House for several years. The chamber conducted business in this miniature building on McKinney Street, allowing six-minute Visitor Information Parking (VIP). The chamber moved into its current facility at the corner of Parkway Street and Carroll Boulevard in 1975. (Courtesy of DRC.)

Pat Boone left Denton in 1956 after studying music at North Texas State College for one year. In 1958, he capitalized on his popularity as a movie and television star to partner in launching a restaurant on University Drive called Pat Boone Country Inn. The restaurant closed in 1962. Meridian Bank is the latest of several financial institutions that have occupied this location. (Courtesy of DRC.)

Considered to be one of the most striking structures in Denton and compared to renowned concert halls around the world, the Murchison Performing Arts Center is home to the University of North Texas College of Music. The acoustics in Winspear Performance Hall are superb due to its unique construction. It is a great improvement over the old auditorium building used for performances in the 1940s. (Courtesy of DPL.)

The first Piggly Wiggly grocery store opened in 1941, expanding to several stores providing neighborhood services to generations of Denton families "down home, down the street." The town's last Piggly Wiggly closed to tearful shoppers in 2009. Winfree Academy Charter School opened in 2000 to provide an educational setting for 9th to 12th grade students needing an alternative to a traditional school environment. (Courtesy of DRC.)

Fred Douglas Moore, principal of the Fred Douglass School since 1915, served as principal of the school renamed in his honor. Fred Moore School opened in 1949 and closed its high school in 1967 and elementary school in 1969. The school now operates as the alternative high school for the Denton Independent School District. (Courtesy of DRC.)

Joe and Alice (Clark) Skinner, seen below on Bell Avenue in Quakertown, were married on Christmas Day 1913. The following spring, the elderly newlyweds moved to 805 Bell Avenue, where Joe Skinner operated a shoe and toy repair shop in a building on the south end of the property. Old Main, on the College of Industrial Arts (now Texas Woman's University) campus, is in the background of both photographs. (Courtesy of Mike Cochran.)

The members of the Household of Ruth women's societal organization are shown here on a bridge crossing the lower branch of Pecan Creek on Oakland Avenue just north of McKinney Street in Quakertown. The home of Harriet Hampton can be seen in the background on the left. The area is a beautiful park setting today with the creek still running through it. (Courtesy of Mike Cochran.)

Oran E. Monroe and Wilburn Pearson moved from Gainesville in 1931 and purchased Pearlstone-Bolton Grocery Company. They soon formed Monroe-Pearson Wholesale Grocery Company, which operated until 1979. Fantasia Fans Fireplaces, a wholesaler of ceiling fans, fireplaces, and stoves, now occupies the warehouse space. (Courtesy of Louise Vanderhoff.)

The Graham Mill and Elevator Company, built in 1900, became Kimbell-Diamond Milling in 1934. A rare view of the engine room of the old mill is shown at far right. A 1967 fire destroyed the flour mill and grain elevator, which was producing 120,000 pounds of flour a day. The remaining structure underwent adaptive reuse in 1996 as the offices of Tim Beaty Builders. (Courtesy of Louise Vanderhoff.)

Despite the lack of advance notice, around 200 people attended a 1965 impromptu fly-in at Hartlee Field, a former training facility for US Army Air Force liaison pilots. Hartlee Field continued to be used as a private instruction airfield. Former flight instructors and their students attended reunions every year, the last of which was in 2009. Now privately owned, flight has mostly ceased on the unpaved airstrip. (Then photograph courtesy of Smith and Etha Kiker, now photograph courtesy of *Hartlee Times*.)

CHAPTER 4

Times, They Are Changing

This July 4, 1899, parade on the downtown square features the Ariel Club riding in the "tally-ho" wagon in the center of the picture. The women are Helen Ponder, Anna Clare Walden, Clara Hann, Johnnie Mae Hann, and Miss Lee Williams. Alvin C. Owsley and his children are riding in the pony cart behind the Ariel Club.

O'Neil Ford designed the bathhouse for the Denton Municipal Swimming Pool in 1965. The wooden bathhouse was demolished in 1993 and replaced with a brick structure that integrated Ford's ceramic fixtures. Ironically, this was the same year that the city hall, Civic Center, and the municipal pool were named the O'Neil Ford Civic Complex. Water Works Park, opened at Sherman Drive in summer 2003, features four giant slides, a pool, a continuous flowing river, a volleyball court, an amphitheater, picnic pavilions, and a natatorium. (Courtesy of DRC.)

Ginger Rogers's 1944 movie *Lady in the Dark, the Minx in Mink Who Had a Yen for Men*, helped date this photograph of the city's wastepaper collection for the war effort, located at the corner of Cedar and West Oak Streets. The current city recycling centers recover food and beverage cartons, boxes, plastic and glass bottles, and aluminum and tin cans for reuse, and yard waste to be converted into Dyno Dirt brand soil, compost, and mulch. (Courtesy of DRC.)

Denton began celebrating its 100th anniversary of the founding of the city on April 22, 1957, with a parade around the downtown square. That tradition still remains today with the fanfare of the North Texas State Fair Parade held in August. Horses and wagons have always played an important role in parades in this Wild West city. (Courtesy of DPL.)

The North Texas State Fair began as the Denton County Fair in 1928. The fairgrounds received a permanent home off Carroll Boulevard in 1948. The event became the North Texas State Fair and Rodeo in 1989 when it brought the first Professional Rodeo Cowboys Association rodeo competition to the fair. The rodeo still comes to town and provides thrills and spills for cowboys and fans alike.

The first Spring Fling Festival was held in April 1980 at the fairgrounds. Spring Fling featured celebrities such as "Mean Joe" Green and attracted an estimated 30,000 visitors. The Denton Arts & Jazz Festival was founded in 1991 and has hosted more than 300,000 visitors annually. Carol Short, director of the Denton Festival Foundation, is shown here with jazz greats "Blue" Lou Marini, Tom "Bones" Malone, and Marvin Stamm and the Leon Breeden Tribute Band. (Courtesy of DRC.)

Dogs have always held a special place in Denton residents' lives, as seen in this 1903 photograph of Gentry Thompson and his dog riding in one of Denton's earliest automobiles. Dog Days of Denton is Texas's original celebration for pooches and their people, featuring entertainment, doggy demonstrations, canine contests, arts and crafts, pet care products, and services. Shown here are Akayla and Baxter with their human, DyAnn Matthews. (Courtesy of DPL.)

Fouts Field, opened in 1952, was named in 1954 in honor of Theron J. Fouts, former University of North Texas football coach and athletic director. A new stadium, designed for the University of North Texas by the same firm that designed Cowboys Stadium and the Texas Rangers Ballpark at Arlington, is built in part with recycled materials utilizing solar panels and wind turbines to provide some of the stadium's power needs. (Courtesy of UNT.)

The Denton Municipal Airport was completed in 1947 with a single concrete runway 4,150 feet in length and 150 feet wide. The airport terminal building, designed by O'Neil Ford, was dedicated in 1965 with a crowd of 6,000 in attendance. The Denton Air Show draws thousands of spectators to its annual event featuring aerial entertainment and equipment. (Courtesy of DRC.)

In 1924, the Texas Interurban Railway provided transportation between Denton and Dallas along the Missouri, Kansas & Texas Railroad (MKT) tracks. Train service was derailed in the early 1930s due to the prevalence of the automobile and the Great Depression. Eighty years later, Denton is bringing back train transportation between Denton and Dallas with the A-train. It is ironic that the same reasons for the death of rail transportation are what are reviving it. (Courtesy of Dr. Johnnie Myers.)

This 1940s photograph of Ariel Club members was taken in front of the Woman's Club Building, which was completed in 1928 with funds raised by the City Federation of Women's Clubs. Ladies of the club played a prominent role in community improvement activities. These current women's club members, sans hats, pose in front of the Woman's Club Building. (Courtesy of Lucile Hutchinson.)

The Courthouse-on-the-Square Museum first occupied the second floor courtroom of the historical courthouse in 1979 and moved to the first floor in early 1988. The Courthouse Museum's main gallery is still on the first floor, with more exhibits featured throughout the rest of the building. The Denton County Historical Commission and museum staff offices and museum archives occupy the remainder of the basement and first floor. (Courtesy of DRC.)

In the background of this 1960s picture are the parallel streets of Mulberry and Sycamore Streets with a row of homes that were torn down to make way for commercial development. The area became the Historical Park of Denton County, which is being developed with historically significant structures that are restored by the Denton County Historical Commission with the help of the Historical Park Foundation of Denton County. (Courtesy of DRC.)

Samuel A. Bayless and his wife, Mary, purchased a two-room farmhouse in 1884, and in 1898, they added this Victorian Queen Anne–style house. After Samuel died in 1919, Mary sold the house in 1920 to R.L. Selby Sr. and his wife, Mary. The Selby family retained ownership until 1970. The house was moved in 1998 to the Historical Park of Denton County. After restoration, the Bayless-Selby House Museum opened in 2001. (Courtesy of City of Denton.)

Originally constructed in 1904 in the African American community of Quakertown, this house was moved by C. Ross Hembry to Solomon Hill in 1922 when the citizens of Denton voted to make the Quakertown area into a park. In 2004, the house was moved to the Historical Park and opened in 2009 as the award-winning Denton County African American Museum.

The 1904 servants' quarters for the Benjamin Spencer family home in Lewisville were occupied by their maid Maggie and her husband, Julian Hembry. This photograph shows Annie Spencer in the early 1900s keeping watch over her hired help. The building was moved to the Historical Park in 2008 and renovated into a welcome center depicting some of the history of the main house, family, and the town of Lewisville. (Courtesy of Don Epperson.)

This building served as the Elm Ridge United Methodist Church in Navo from 1920 until 1986 when it was replaced by a new church structure. The church's roots go back to 1886. The Denton County Historical Commission will restore the old church building in the Historical Park of Denton County to be used again as a community room and wedding chapel. (Courtesy of Melvena Noles)

Denton purchased a Peter Pirsch hook and ladder fire truck in 1935. The truck, known as Old No. 14, was in service until the 1970s. The Denton County Historical Commission acquired the truck in 1984. Old No. 14 is being restored to reside in a firehouse museum in the Historical Park of Denton County. Old No.14 is pictured in front of the former city hall that also served as the downtown fire station.

About the Authors

Kim Cupit, curator of collections, and Georgia Caraway, former director, have worked together for 13 years for Denton County museums. Kim holds a bachelors degree in history from Austin College in Sherman, and Georgia earned a doctorate in higher education administration from the University of North Texas in Denton. Kim and Georgia have spent their museum careers developing Denton County Museums, including the Courthouse Museum and the Historical Park of Denton County. They have written two other historical photographic books for Arcadia Publishing, Images of America: *Denton* and Postcard History Series: *Denton County*. A fourth Arcadia book, *African Americans in Denton County*, is scheduled for publication in 2013.